I0012279

NIST 800-137: An Introduction to Information Security Continuous Monitoring (ISCM)

Mark A. Russo, CISSP-ISSAP

Syber-Risk.com

NIST 800-137: An Introduction to Information Security-Continuous Monitoring by Mark A. Russo

Copyright © 2019 Syber-Risk.com LLC. All rights reserved.

Printed in the United States of America.

January 2019:   First Edition

Revision History for the First Edition
2019:   First Release

On September 1, 2018, We Launched the *Most Extensive* Cybersecurity Blog Site on the Web

This is the major resource of everything "Cyber."
"The good, the bad, and the ugly of cybersecurity all in one place."

Join us at https://cybersentinel.tech

This free resource is available to everyone interested in the fate and future of cybersecurity in the 21st Century

DEDICATION

This book is dedicated to the cybersecurity men and women of the Department of Defense and US Cybercommand that protect and defend the Information Systems of this great Nation...we salute you!

NIST 800-137: An Introduction to Information Security Continuous Monitoring (ISCM)

Table of Contents

Cybersecurity Continuous Monitoring (CCM)

This book is written as a beginner's guide to the challenges and solutions of CCM as proscribed by the National Institute of Standards and Technology (NIST). CCM is to be that final step in the Risk Management Framework (RMF) process.

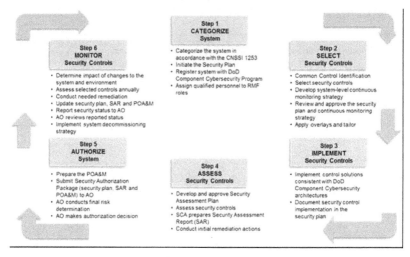

RMF for Information Systems (IS)

Once you have completed all the five preceding steps, you will enter Step 6, Continuous Monitoring. Some of this can be done manually, but the objective is to automate the process to alert System Owner's of critical changes in the architecture that afford vulnerabilities and avenues of approach for threats; threats that may include Insider Threats and nation-state actors such as Russia, China, and Iran. CCM is on the horizon, yet we are years from attaining true CCM as described in this book.

This book will introduce to the major frameworks designed to support this next phase to CCM. The objective is to increase your understanding and ability to affect future change. A change that will stifle the "bad guys" and protect your precious networks and data. This is not a book about shortcuts, but methods and means that will protect us all from the global cyber-threats.

It's Not About Shortcuts

Cybersecurity is not about shortcuts. There are no easy solutions to years of leaders demurring their responsibility to address the growing threats in cyberspace. We hoped that the 2015 Office of Personnel Management (OPM) breach several years ago would herald the needed focus, energy and funding to quash the bad-guys. That has proven an empty hope where leaders have abrogated their responsibility to lead in cyberspace. The "holy grail" solution of Continuous Monitoring (CCM) has been the most misunderstood solution where too many shortcuts are perpetrated by numerous federal agencies and the private sector to create an illusion of success. This paper is specifically written to help leaders better understand what constitutes a true statement of: "we have continuous monitoring." This is not about shortcuts. This is about education, training, and understanding at the highest leadership levels that cybersecurity is not a technical issue, but a leadership issue.

The Committee on National Security Systems defines CCM as: "[t]he processes implemented to maintain current security status for one or more information systems on which the operational mission of the enterprise depends," (CNSS, 2010). CCM has been described as the holistic solution of end-to-end cybersecurity coverage and the answer to providing an effective global Risk Management (RM) solution. It promises the elimination of the 3-year recertification cycle that has been the bane of cybersecurity professionals.

For CCM to become a reality for any agency, it must meet the measures and expectations as defined in National Institute of Standards and Technology (NIST) Special Publication (SP) 800-137, Information Security Continuous Monitoring for Federal Information Systems and Organizations. "Continuous monitoring has evolved as a best practice for managing risk on an ongoing basis," (SANS Institute, 2016); it is an instrument that supports effective, continual, and recurring RM assurances. For any agency to truly espouse it has attained full CCM compliance, it must be able to coordinate all the described major elements as found in NIST SP 800-137.

CCM is not just the passive visibility pieces, but also includes the active efforts of vulnerability scanning, threat alert, reduction, mitigation, or elimination of a dynamic Information Technology (IT) environment. The Department of Homeland Security (DHS) has couched its approach to CCM more holistically. Their program to protect government networks is more aptly called: "Continuous Diagnostics and Monitoring" or CDM and includes a need to react to an active network attacker. "The ability to make IT networks, end-points and applications visible; to identify malicious activity; and, to respond [emphasis added] immediately is critical to defending information systems and networks," (Sann, 2016).

Another description of CCM can be found in NIST's CAESARS Framework Extension: An Enterprise Continuous Monitoring Technical Reference Model (Second Draft). It defines its essential characteristics within the concept of "Continuous Security Monitoring." It is described as a "...risk management approach to Cybersecurity that maintains a picture of an organization's security posture, provides visibility into assets, leverages use of automated data feeds, monitors effectiveness of security controls, and enables prioritization of remedies," (NIST, 2012); it must demonstrate visibility, data feeds, measures of effectiveness and allow for solutions. It provides another description of what should be demonstrated to ensure full CCM designation under the NIST standard.

The US government's Federal Risk and Authorization Management Program (Fed-RAMP) has defined similar CCM goals. These objectives are all key outcomes of a successful CCM implementation. Its "... goal[s]...[are] to provide: (i) operational visibility; (ii) annual self-attestations on security control implementations; (iii) managed change control; (iv) and attendance to incident response duties," (GSA, 2012). These objectives, while not explicit to NIST SP 800-37, are well-aligned with the desires of an effective and complete solution.

RMF creates the structure and documentation needs of CCM; it represents the specific implementation and oversight of Information Security (IS) within an IT environment. It supports the general activity of RM within an agency. (See Figure 1 below). The RMF "... describes a disciplined and structured process that integrates information security and risk management activities into the system development life cycle," (NIST-B, 2011). RMF is the structure that both describes and relies upon CCM as its risk oversight and effectiveness mechanism between IS and RM.

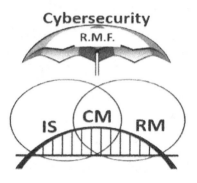

Figure 1. CM "bridges" Information Security and Risk Management

This book provides a conceptual framework to address how an agency would approach identifying a true CCM solution through NIST SP 800-137. It discusses the additional need to align component requirements with the "*11 Security Automation Domains*" that are necessary to implement true CCM. (See Figure 2 below). It is through the complete implementation and integration with the other described components—See Figure 3 below--that an organization can correctly state it has achieved CCM.

Figure 2. The 11 Security Automation Domains (NIST, 2011)

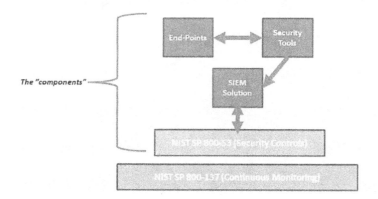

Figure 3. The "Components" of an Effective Continuous Monitoring

Cybersecurity Continuous Monitoring – First Generation

For CCM to be effective and genuine, it must align end-point visibility with security monitoring tools. This includes security monitoring tools with connectivity to "end-points" such as laptops, desktops, servers, routers, firewalls, etc. Additionally, these must work with a highly integrated Security Information and Event Management (SIEM) device. The other "component" is a clear linkage between the end-points, security monitoring tools, and the SIEM appliance, working with the *Security Automation Domains* (See Figure 2). These would include, for example, the areas of malware detection, asset and event management. CCM must first address these collective components to create a "First Generation" instantiation.

More specifically, a SIEM appliance provides the central core data processing capabilities to effectively coordinate all the inputs and outputs from across the IT enterprise. It manages the data integration and interpretation of all CCM components. And, it provides the necessary visibility and intelligence for an active incident response capability.

End-point devices must be persistently visible to the applicable security devices. Together, these parts must align with the respective security controls as described in NIST SP 800-53. The selected SIEM tool must be able to accept these inputs and analyze them against defined security policy settings, recurring vulnerability scans, signature-based threats, and heuristic/activity-based analyses to ensure the environment's security posture. The outputs of the SIEM must support the further visibility of the IT environment, conduct and disseminate vital intelligence, and alert leadership to any ongoing or imminent dangers. The expression above is designed to provide a conceptual representation of the cybersecurity professional attempting to ascertain effective CCM implementation or to develop a complete CCM answer for an agency or corporation.

Additionally, the SIEM must distribute data feeds in near-real time to analysts and key leaders. It provides for multi-level "dashboard" data streams and issues alert based upon prescribed policy settings. Once these base, First Generation functionalities are consistently aligning with the Security Automation Domains, then an organization or corporation can definitively express it meets the requirements of CCM.

End-Points

It is necessary to identify hardware and software configuration items that must be known and constantly traceable before implementing CCM within an enterprise IT environment. End-point visibility is not the hardware devices, but the baseline software of each hardware device on the network.

Configuration Management is also a foundational requirement for any organization's security posture. Soundly implemented Configuration Management must be the basis of any complete CM implementation. At the beginning of any IS effort, cyber-professionals must know the current "as-is" hardware and software component state within the enterprise. End-points must be protected and monitored because they are the most valuable target for would-be hackers and cyber-thieves.

Configuration Management provides the baseline that establishes a means to identify potential compromise between the enterprise's end-points and the requisite security tools. "Organizations with a robust and effective [Configuration Management] process need to consider information security implications concerning the development and operation of information systems including hardware, software, applications, and documentation," (NIST-A, 2011).

The RMF requires the categorization of systems and data as high, moderate, or low regarding risk. The Federal Information Processing Standards (FIPS) Publication 199 methodology is typically used to establish data sensitivity levels in the federal government. FIPS 199 aids the cybersecurity professional in determining data protection standards of both end-points and the data stored in these respective parts. For example, a system that collects and retains sensitive data, such as financial information, requires a greater level of security. It is important that end-points are recognized as repositories of highly valued data to cyber-threats.

Further, cyber-security professionals must be constantly aware of the "...administrative and technological costs of offering a high degree of protection for all federal systems...," (Ross, Katzke, & Toth, 2005). This is not a matter of recognizing the physical end-point alone but the value and associated costs of the virtual data stored, monitored, and protected on a continual basis. FIPS 199 assists system owners in determining whether a higher level of protection is warranted, with higher associated costs, based upon an overall FIPS 199 evaluation.

Security Tools

Security monitoring tools must identify in near-real time an active threat. Examples include anti-virus or anti-malware applications used to monitor network and end-point activities. Products like McAfee and Symantec provide enterprise capabilities that help to identify and reduce threats.

Other security tools would address in whole or part the remaining NIST Security Automation Domains. These would include, for example, tools to provide asset visibility, vulnerability detection, patch management updates, etc. But it is also critical to recognize that even the best current security tools are not necessarily capable of defending against all attacks. New malware or zero-day attacks pose continual challenges to the cybersecurity workforce.

For example, DHS's EINSTEIN system would not have stopped the 2015 Office of Personnel Management breach. Even DHS's latest iteration of EINSTEIN, EINSTEIN 3, an advanced network monitoring and response system designed to protect federal governments' networks, would not have stopped that attack. "...EINSTEIN 3 would not have been able to catch a threat that [had] no known footprints, according to multiple industry experts," (Sternstein, 2015).

Not until there are a much greater integration and availability of cross-cutting intelligence and more capable security tools, can any single security tool ever be fully effective. The need for multiple security monitoring tools that provide "defense in depth" may be a better protective strategy. However, with multiple tools monitoring the same Security Automation Domains, such an approach will certainly increase the costs of maintaining a secure agency or corporate IT environment. A determination of Return on Investment (ROI) balanced against a well-defined threat risk scoring approach is further needed at all levels of the federal and corporate IT workspace.

Security Controls

"Organizations are required to adequately mitigate the risk arising from the use of information and information systems in the execution of missions and business functions," (NIST, 2013). This is accomplished by the selection and implementation of NIST SP 800-53, Revision 4, described security controls. (See Figure 4 below). They are organized into eighteen families to address sub-set security areas such as access control, physical security, incident response, etc. The use of these controls is typically tailored to the security categorization by the respective system owner relying upon FIPS 199 categorization standards. A higher security categorization requires the greater implementation of these controls.

ID	FAMILY	ID	FAMILY
AC	Access Control	MP	Media Protection
AT	Awareness and Training	PE	Physical and Environmental Protection
AU	Audit and Accountability	PL	Planning
CA	Security Assessment and Authorization	PS	Personnel Security
CM	Configuration Management	RA	Risk Assessment
CP	Contingency Planning	SA	System and Services Acquisition
IA	Identification and Authentication	SC	System and Communications Protection
IR	Incident Response	SI	System and Information Integrity
MA	Maintenance	PM	Program Management

Figure 4. Security Control Identifiers and Family Names, (NIST, 2013)

Security Information and Event Management (SIEM) Solutions

The SIEM tool plays a pivotal role in any viable "First Generation" implementation. Based on NIST and DHS guidance, an effective SIEM appliance must provide the following functionalities:

- "Aggregate data from "across a diverse set" of security tool sources;
- Analyze the multi-source data;
- Engage in explorations of data based on changing needs
- Make quantitative use of data for security (not just reporting) purposes including the development and use of risk scores; and
- Maintain actionable awareness of the changing security situation on a real-time basis," (Levinson, 2011).

"Effectiveness is further enhanced when the output is formatted to provide information that is specific, measurable, actionable, relevant, and timely," (NIST, 2011). The SIEM device is the vital core of a full solution that collects, analyzes, and alerts the cyber-professional of potential and actual dangers in their environment.

There are several major SIEM solutions that can effectively meet the requirements of NIST SP 800-137. They include products, for example, IBM® Security, Splunk®, and Hewlett Packard's® ArcSight® products.

For example, Logrhythm ® was highly rated in the 2014 SIEM evaluation. Logrhythm® provided network event monitoring and alerts of potential security compromises. The implementation of an enterprise-grade SIEM solution is necessary to meet growing cybersecurity requirements for auditing of security logs and capabilities to respond to cyber-incidents. SIEM products will continue to play a critical and evolving role in the demands for "…increased security and rapid response to events throughout the network," (McAfee® Foundstone Professional Services®, 2013). Improvements and upgrades of SIEM tools are critical to providing a more highly responsive capability for future generations of these appliances in the marketplace.

Next Generations

Future generations of CCM would include specific expanded capabilities and functionalities of the SIEM device. These second generation and beyond evolutions would be more effective solutions in future dynamic and hostile network environments. Such advancements might also include increased access to a greater pool of threat database signature repositories or more expansive heuristics that could identify active anomalies within a target network.

Another futuristic capability might include the use of Artificial Intelligence (AI). Improved capabilities of a SIEM appliance with AI augmentation would further enhance human threat analysis and provide for more automated responsiveness. "The concept of predictive analysis involves using statistical methods and decision tools that analyze current and historical data to make predictions about future events...," (SANS Institute). The next generation would boost human response times and abilities to defend against attacks in a matter of milli-seconds vice hours.

Finally, in describing the next generations of CCM, it is not only imperative to expand data, informational and intelligence inputs for new and more capable SIEM products, but that input and corresponding data sets must also be fully vetted for completeness and accuracy. Increased access to signature and heuristic activity-based analysis databases would provide greater risk reduction. Greater support from private industry and the Intelligence Community would also be major improvements for Agencies that are constantly struggling against a more-capable and better-resourced threat.

CCM will not be a reality until vendors and agencies can integrate the right people, processes, and technologies. "Security needs to be positioned as an enabler of the organization—it must take its place alongside human resources, financial resources, sound business processes and strategies, information technology, and intellectual capital as the elements of success for accomplishing the mission," (Caralli, 2004). CCM is not just a technical solution. It requires capable organizations with trained personnel, creating effective policies and procedures with the requisite technologies to stay ahead of the growing threats in cyberspace.

Figure 6 below provides a graphic depiction of what CCM components are needed to create a holistic NIST SP 800-137-compliant solution; this demonstrates the First-Generation representation. There are numerous vendors describing that they have the "holy grail" solution, but until they can prove they meet this description in total, it is unlikely they have a complete implementation of a thorough CCM solution yet.

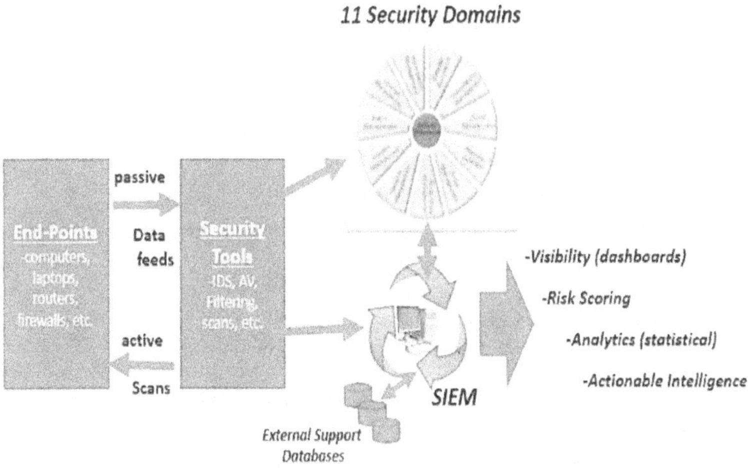

11 Security Domains

passive

End-Points
-computers,
laptops,
routers,
firewalls, etc.

Data
feeds

active

Scans

Security Tools
-IDS, AV,
Filtering,
scans, etc.

External Support Databases

SIEM

-*Visibility (dashboards)*

-*Risk Scoring*

-*Analytics (statistical)*

-*Actionable Intelligence*

Figure 6. First Generation Continuous Monitoring

Endnotes

Balakrishnan, B. (2015, October 6). *Insider Threat Mitigation Guidance* . Retrieved from SANS Institute Infosec Reading Room: https://www.sans.org/reading-room/whitepapers/monitoring/insider-threat-mitigation-guidance-36307

Caralli, R. A. (2004, December). *Managing Enterprise Security (CMU/SEI-2004-TN-046).* Retrieved from Software Engineering Institute: http://www.sei.cmu.edu/reports/04tn046.pdf

Committee on National Security Systems. (2010, April 26). *National Information Assurance (IA) Glossary.* Retrieved from National Counterintelligence & Security Center: http://www.ncsc.gov/nittf/docs/CNSSI-4009_National_Information_Assurance.pdf

Department of Defense. (2014, March 12). *DOD Instructions 8510.01: Risk Management Framework (RMF) for DoD Information Technology (IT).* Retrieved from Defense Technical Information Center (DTIC): http://www.dtic.mil/whs/directives/corres/pdf/851001_2014.pdf

GSA. (2012, January 27). *Continuous Monitoring Strategy & Guide, v1.1.* Retrieved from General Services Administration: http://www.gsa.gov/graphics/staffoffices/Continuous_Monitoring_Strategy_Guide_072712.pdf

Joint Medical Logistics Functional Development Center. (2015). JMLFDC Continuous Monitoring Strategy Plan and Procedure. Ft Detrick, MD.

Kavanagh, K. M., Nicolett, M., & Rochford, O. (2014, June 25). *Magic Quadrant for Security Information and Event Management.* Retrieved from Gartner: http://www.gartner.com/technology/reprints.do?id=1-1W8AO4W&ct=140627&st=sb&mkt_tok=3RkMMJWWfF9wsRolsqrJcO%2FhmjTEU5z17u8lWa%2B0gYkz2EFye%2BLIHETpodcMTcVkNb%2FYDBceEJhqyQJxPr3FKdANz8JpRhnqAA%3D%3D

Kolenko, M. M. (2016, February 18). *SPECIAL-The Human Element of Cybersecurity*. Retrieved from Homeland Security Today.US: http://www.hstoday.us/briefings/industry-news/single-article/special-the-human-element-of-cybersecurity/54008efd46e93863f54db0f7352dde2c.html

Levinson, B. (2011, October). *Federal Cybersecurity Best Practices Study: Information Security Continuous Monitoring.* Retrieved from Center for Regulatory Effectiveness: http://www.thecre.com/fisma/wp-content/uploads/2011/10/Federal-Cybersecurity-Best-Practice.ISCM_2.pdf

McAfee® Foundstone® Professional Services. (2013). *McAfee.* Retrieved from White Paper: Creating and Maintaining a SOC: http://www.mcafee.com/us/resources/white-papers/foundstone/wp-creating-maintaining-soc.pdf

NIST. (2011-A, August). *NIST SP 800-128: Guide for Security-Focused Configuration Management of Information Systems.* Retrieved from NIST Computer Security Resource Center: http://csrc.nist.gov/publications/nistpubs/800-128/sp800-128.pdf

NIST. (2011-B, September). *Special Publication 800-137: Information Security Continuous Monitoring (ISCM) for Federal Information Systems and Organizations.* Retrieved from NIST Computer Security Resource Center: http://csrc.nist.gov/publications/nistpubs/800-137/SP800-137-Final.pdf

NIST. (2012, January). *NIST Interagency Report 7756: CAESARS Framework Extension: An Enterprise Continuous Monitoring Technical Reference Model (Second Draft),* . Retrieved from NIST Computer Resource Security Center: http://csrc.nist.gov/publications/drafts/nistir-7756/Draft-NISTIR-7756_second-public-draft.pdf

NIST. (2013, April). *NIST SP 800-53, Rev 4: Security and Privacy Controls for Federal Information Systems* . Retrieved from NIST: http://nvlpubs.nist.gov/nistpubs/SpecialPublications/NIST.SP.800-53r4.pdf

Ross, R., Katzke, S., & Toth, P. (2005, October 17). *The New FISMA Standards and Guidelines Changing the Dynamic of Information Security for the Federal Government.* Retrieved from Information Technology Promotion Agency of Japan: https://www.ipa.go.jp/files/000015362.pdf

Sann, W. (2016, January 8). *The Key Missing Piece of Your Cyber Strategy? Visibility.* Retrieved from Nextgov: http://www.nextgov.com/technology-news/tech-insider/2016/01/key-missing-element-your-cyber-strategy-visibility/124974/

SANS Institute. (2016, March 6). *Beyond Continuous Monitoring: Threat Modeling for Real-time Response.* Retrieved from SANS Institute: http://www.sans.org/reading-room/whitepapers/analyst/continuous-monitoring-threat-modeling-real-time-response-35185

Sternstein, A. (2015, January 6). *OPM Hackers Skirted Cutting-Edge Intrusion Detection System, Official Says* . Retrieved from Nextgov: http://www.nextgov.com/cybersecurity/2015/06/opm-hackers-skirted-cutting-edge-interior-intrusion-detection-official-says/114649/

Appendix A—Relevant Terms

Audit log.
: A chronological record of information system activities, including records of system accesses and operations performed in a given period.

Authentication.
: Verifying the identity of a user, process, or device, often as a prerequisite to allowing access to resources in an information system.

Availability.
: Ensuring timely and reliable access to and use of information.

Baseline Configuration.
: A documented set of specifications for an information system, or a configuration item within a system, that has been formally reviewed and agreed on at a given point in time, and which can be changed only through change control procedures.

Blacklisting.
: The process used to identify: (i) software programs that are not authorized to execute on an information system; or (ii) prohibited websites.

Confidentiality.
: Preserving authorized restrictions on information access and disclosure, including means for protecting personal privacy and proprietary information.

Configuration Management.
: A collection of activities focused on establishing and maintaining the integrity of information technology products and information systems, through control of processes for initializing, changing, and monitoring the configurations of those products and systems throughout the system development life cycle.

Controlled Unclassified Information (CUI/CDI).
: Information that law, regulation, or governmentwide policy requires to have safeguarding or disseminating controls, excluding information that is classified under Executive Order 13526, Classified National Security Information, December 29, 2009, or any predecessor or successor order, or the Atomic Energy Act of 1954, as amended.

Cybersecurity
: The process of protecting information by preventing, detecting, and responding to attacks.

Cybersecurity Event
: A cybersecurity change that *may* have an impact on organizational operations (including mission, capabilities, or reputation).

Cybersecurity Incident	A cybersecurity event that has been determined to have an impact on the organization prompting the need for response and recovery.
External network.	A network not controlled by the company.
FIPS-validated cryptography.	
	A cryptographic module validated by the Cryptographic Module Validation Program (CMVP) to meet requirements specified in FIPS Publication 140-2 (as amended). As a prerequisite to CMVP validation, the cryptographic module is required to employ a cryptographic algorithm implementation that has successfully passed validation testing by the Cryptographic Algorithm Validation Program (CAVP).
Hardware.	The physical components of an information system.
Incident.	An occurrence that actually or potentially jeopardizes the confidentiality, integrity, or availability of an information system or the information the system processes, stores, or transmits or that constitutes a violation or imminent threat of violation of security policies, security procedures, or acceptable use policies.
Information Security.	The protection of information and information systems from unauthorized access, use, disclosure, disruption, modification, or destruction to provide confidentiality, integrity, and availability.
Information System.	A discrete set of information resources organized for the collection, processing, maintenance, use, sharing, dissemination, or disposition of information.
Information Technology.	Any equipment or interconnected system or subsystem of equipment that is used in the automatic acquisition, storage, manipulation, management, movement, control, display, switching, interchange, transmission, or reception of data or information by the executive agency. It includes computers, ancillary equipment, software, firmware, and similar procedures, services (including support services), and related resources.
Integrity.	Guarding against improper information modification or destruction and includes ensuring information non-repudiation and authenticity.

Internal Network.	A network where: (i) the establishment, maintenance, and provisioning of security controls are under the direct control of organizational employees or contractors; or (ii) cryptographic encapsulation or similar security technology implemented between organization-controlled endpoints, provides the same effect (at least about confidentiality and integrity).
Malicious Code.	Software intended to perform an unauthorized process that will have adverse impact on the confidentiality, integrity, or availability of an information system. A virus, worm, Trojan horse, or other code-based entity that infects a host. Spyware and some forms of adware are also examples of malicious code.
Media.	Physical devices or writing surfaces including, but not limited to, magnetic tapes, optical disks, magnetic disks, and printouts (but not including display media) onto which information is recorded, stored, or printed within an information system.
Mobile Code.	Software programs or parts of programs obtained from remote information systems, transmitted across a network, and executed on a local information system without explicit installation or execution by the recipient.
Mobile device.	A portable computing device that: (i) has a small form factor such that it can easily be carried by a single individual; (ii) is designed to operate without a physical connection (e.g., wirelessly transmit or receive information); (iii) possesses local, nonremovable or removable data storage; and (iv) includes a self-contained power source. Mobile devices may also include voice communication capabilities, on-board sensors that allow the devices to capture information, and/or built-in features for synchronizing local data with remote locations. Examples include smartphones, tablets, and E-readers.
Multifactor Authentication.	Authentication using two or more different factors to achieve authentication. Factors include: (i) something you know (e.g., password/PIN); (ii) something you have (e.g., cryptographic identification device, token); or (iii) something you are (e.g., biometric).
Nonfederal Information System.	
	An information system that does not meet the criteria for a federal information system. nonfederal organization.

Network.	Information system(s) implemented with a collection of interconnected components. Such components may include routers, hubs, cabling, telecommunications controllers, key distribution centers, and technical control devices.
Portable storage device.	An information system component that can be inserted into and removed from an information system, and that is used to store data or information (e.g., text, video, audio, and/or image data). Such components are typically implemented on magnetic, optical, or solid-state devices (e.g., floppy disks, compact/digital video disks, flash/thumb drives, external hard disk drives, and flash memory cards/drives that contain nonvolatile memory).
Privileged Account.	An information system account with authorizations of a privileged user.
Privileged User.	A user that is authorized (and therefore, trusted) to perform security-relevant functions that ordinary users are not authorized to perform.
Remote Access.	Access to an organizational information system by a user (or a process acting on behalf of a user) communicating through an external network (e.g., the Internet).
Risk.	A measure of the extent to which an entity is threatened by a potential circumstance or event, and typically a function of: (i) the adverse impacts that would arise if the circumstance or event occurs; and (ii) the likelihood of occurrence. Information system-related security risks are those risks that arise from the loss of confidentiality, integrity, or availability of information or information systems and reflect the potential adverse impacts to organizational operations (including mission, functions, image, or reputation), organizational assets, individuals, other organizations, and the Nation.
Sanitization.	Actions taken to render data written on media unrecoverable by both ordinary and, for some forms of sanitization, extraordinary means. Process to remove information from media such that data recovery is not possible. It includes removing all classified labels, markings, and activity logs.
Security Control.	A safeguard or countermeasure prescribed for an information system or an organization designed to protect the confidentiality, integrity, and availability of its information and to meet a set of defined security requirements.

Security Control Assessment.

> The testing or evaluation of security controls to determine the extent to which the controls are implemented correctly, operating as intended, and producing the desired

Security Functions.

> The hardware, software, and/or firmware of the information system responsible for enforcing the system security policy and supporting the isolation of code and data on which the protection is based.

Threat.

> Any circumstance or event with the potential to adversely impact organizational operations (including mission, functions, image, or reputation), organizational assets, individuals, other organizations, or the Nation through an information system via unauthorized access, destruction, disclosure, modification of information, and/or denial of service.

Whitelisting.

> The process used to identify: (i) software programs that are authorized to execute on an information system.

Appendix B—Continuous Monitoring Plan (ConMon)Template

The E-Government Act of 2002 (Public Law 107-347) recognized the importance of information security to the economic and national security interests of the United States. Title III of the E-Government Act, Federal Information Security Management Act of 2002 (FISMA), tasked the National Institute of Standards and Technology (NIST) with responsibilities for standards and guidelines, including the development of:

- Standards to be used by all Federal agencies and supporting contracted workforces to categorize all information and information systems collected or maintained by or on behalf of each agency based on the objectives of providing appropriate levels of information security according to a range of risk levels;

- Guidelines recommending the types of information and information systems to be included in each category; and

- Minimum information security requirements (i.e., management, operational, and technical controls) for information and information systems in each such category.

Every federal information system owner must select and implement a set of security controls from NCF, [FULL TITLE HERE]. Once the controls are implemented and the system authorized to operate, they are monitored continuously under the provisions of the NCF, and every three years the system undergoes a full reauthorization or if approved will comply with a continuous monitoring process. The results of continuous monitoring are reported to the system's Authorizing Official and the organization's Senior Agency Information Security Officer (SAISO) [OR OTHER NAMED, e.g., CISO, CIO, ETC.] on a regular basis. The goal of continuous monitoring is to determine if the security controls in the information system continue to be effective over time and, ultimately, to maintain the system's authorization to operate.

The continuous monitoring process is part of Step 6, Monitor Security Controls, of the Risk Management Framework (RMF) defined by NIST. The purpose of this step in the RMF is to provide oversight and monitoring of the security controls in the information system on an ongoing basis and to inform the Authorizing Official when changes occur that may affect the security of the system. The activities in this step of the RMF, which are described in the Continuous Monitoring Plan, are performed continuously throughout the life cycle of the information system. Re-authorization may be required because of specific changes to the information system or because federal or agency policies require periodic re-authorization of the information system.

**This template can be found at https://cybersentinel.tech

The CCM Template

Purpose

The purpose of this plan is to document the approach used for continuous monitoring and assessing enabled security controls on [DEFINED IT SYSTEM BEING ASSESSED]. This plan includes a listing of security controls to be assessed, the methodology used to select the controls, the prioritization of the controls, and the frequency and method of assessing the controls. It describes how the selected security controls are to be monitored and assessed for compliance and effectiveness. It also specifies where the results of continuous monitoring are reported.

Scope

The scope of this Continuous Monitoring Plan is limited to [THE IT SYSTEM] that is hosted at [PHYSICAL LOCATION/ADDRESS].

Background

A critical aspect of the security authorization process is the post-authorization period involving the continuous monitoring of an information system's security controls (including common controls). Conducting a thorough point-in-time assessment of the security controls in an organizational information system is a necessary but not sufficient condition to demonstrate security due diligence. Effective information security programs should also include a continuous monitoring program to check the status of subsets of the security controls in an information system on an ongoing basis. The ultimate objective of the continuous monitoring program is to determine if the security controls in the information system continue to be effective over time given the inevitable changes that occur in the system hardware, software, firmware, or operational environment.

Continuous monitoring involves the participation of individuals in several organizational job roles. It depends on the following: (a) a comprehensive and robust configuration management process; (b) the ability to perform impact analysis of proposed changes to the information system; (c) the ongoing assessment of security controls, which may identify the need for remediation actions; and (d) the reporting of findings.

The continuous monitoring of security controls, as defined for the RMF, overlaps with "conventional" system performance monitoring and security monitoring that many organizations and system owners use to support operations and operational security. Many of the (existing or planned) system monitoring functions provided by automated tools or monitoring systems will support the continuous monitoring process defined by RMF.

Roles and Responsibilities for Continuous Monitoring

This section defines the roles and responsibilities of key personnel associated with the continuous monitoring of security for [NAMED IT SYSTEM]

The Authorizing Official has an approving role and shall:

- Approve the Continuous Monitoring Plan,
- Accept the residual risk of vulnerabilities found, when deemed appropriate,
- Approve the addition of vulnerabilities to the Plan of Action & Milestones (POAM),
- Approve closure of POAM items, or
- Conduct an Authorization Review for the system and determine whether reauthorization is required.

An Authorizing Official Designated Representative (AODR) may be designated to act on behalf of an Authorizing Official in carrying out and coordinating the required activities associated with security authorization. The AODR may perform the Authorizing Officials duties except for making the authorization decision and signing the associated authorization decision document (i.e., the acceptance of risk to organizational operations and assets, individuals, and other organizations).

The Senior Agency Information Security Officer (SAISO) [OR LIKE SENIOR CYBERSECURITY POSITION] has responsibilities that assist in achieving compliance the NCF. The SENIOR CYBERSECURITY POSITION] has a coordinating role in continuous monitoring and shall:

- Establish, implement, and maintain the organization's continuous monitoring program
- Develop organizational guidance for continuous monitoring of information systems
- Develop configuration guidance for the organization's information technologies
- Consolidate and analyze POAM to determine organizational security weaknesses and deficiencies
- Acquire/develop and maintain automated tools to support security authorization and continuous monitoring
- Provide training on the organization's continuous monitoring process
- Provide support to information owners/information system owners on how to develop and implement continuous monitoring strategies for their information systems, and
- Coordinate organizational common control providers (e.g., external service providers) to ensure that they implement required security controls, assess those controls, and share the assessment results with the clients of the common controls (i.e., the system owners).

The Security Control Assessor (SCA) [AKA, AUDITOR, ASSESSOR, ETC.] shall:

- Participate in the development of the Continuous Monitoring Plan,
- Review the Continuous Monitoring Plan and approve for its submission,
- Assist the ISSO to ensure Continuous Monitoring activities are conducted,
- Conduct the assessment of security controls as defined in the Continuous Monitoring Plan,
- Update the Security Assessment Report (SAR) on a regular basis with the continuous monitoring assessment results, and

- Assist the ISSO to ensure vulnerabilities discovered during the security controls assessment are either corrected or mitigated and that system risk is determined.

The Information System Security Officer (ISSO) monitors system security and supports the other roles. The ISSO shall:

- Assist in the development of the Continuous Monitoring Plan,
- Approve the Continuous Monitoring Plan for submission to the Authorizing Official,
- Ensure Continuous Monitoring assessment is conducted, and
- Ensure that vulnerabilities discovered during the security controls assessment are either corrected or mitigated and tracked to closure, and that system risk is determined,
- Assist the Information System Owner in updating the selection of security controls for the information system when events occur that indicate the baseline set of security controls is no longer adequate to protect the system.

The Information System Owner is responsible for the monitoring process and shall:

- Develop and document a continuous monitoring strategy for each information system with assistance from the ISSO and Security Control Assessor,
- With assistance from the ISSO and Security Control Assessor, assess risk as needed, such as when system/network/environment changes are proposed or implemented, or when new vulnerabilities are discovered,
- Document vulnerabilities and remediation of vulnerabilities,
- With assistance from the ISSO, update the selection of security controls for the information system when events occur that indicate the baseline set of security controls is no longer adequate to protect the system,
- Update authorization documentation package based on continuous monitoring results,
- Prepare and submit security status reports at the organization-defined frequency,
- Review reports from common control providers to verify that the common controls continue to provide adequate protection for the information system.

Configuration Management

Documenting information system changes and evaluating the potential impact those changes may have on the security state of the system is an essential aspect of continuous monitoring. Both continuous monitoring and configuration management (CM) should work harmoniously to ensure that the goals of each process are achieved. The CM process can benefit from continuous system monitoring to ensure that the system is operating as intended and that implemented changes do not adversely impact either the performance or security posture of the system. One activity of continuous system monitoring is to perform configuration verification tests to ensure that the configuration for a given system has not been altered outside of the established CM process. In addition to configuration verification tests, agencies should also perform system audits. Both configuration verification tests and system audits entail an examination of characteristics of the system and supporting documentation to verify that the configuration meets user needs and to ensure the current configuration is the approved system configuration baseline.

It is important to document the proposed or actual changes to the information system or its operational environment and to subsequently determine the impact of those proposed or actual changes on the overall security state of the system. Information systems will typically be in a constant state of change with upgrades to hardware, software, or firmware and possible modifications to the surrounding environments where the systems reside.

Risk Assessment

A change to a system may introduce new vulnerabilities or may interfere with existing security controls. An impact analysis, therefore, should be conducted prior to system modifications to determine if there will be significant impact to the system security posture caused by the changes. If the analysis reveals that there will be a significant impact if the proposed change(s) is made, then additional analysis or testing of the modification may be required, or a security reauthorization may be warranted. If the changes will not significantly impact security status, then the changes should still be assessed (e.g., tested) before moving into production. Continuous monitoring testing priority should be given to controls that have changed.

The general steps of the security impact analysis are as follows:
- Understand the change in a system change request;
- Identify vulnerabilities that the proposed change may introduce;
- Assess risks to the information system, system users, and the organization's mission/business functions;
- Assess security controls that are impacted by the proposed change; for instance, there may be a cascade affect or interference on other security controls;
- Plan safeguards and countermeasures to the identified impacts; and
- Update critical security documentation to reflect the changes made to the information system.

When continuous monitoring identifies a potential problem that needs to be examined (for example, an intrusion prevention system (IPS) detects an attempted change to a data stream not defined in a threat signature database), the following items should be considered:
- Identify impact on other security controls that the problem may be causing.
- Identify any inconsistency(ies) between security policy, procedures, and IT practices that may have been uncovered by the problem.

If such an examination indicates that a change must be made to the system, then the security impact analysis steps above must be followed. Once the impact analysis has validated the need for a change in the system, the system owner may consider doing the following:
- Determine risk level of making the change.

- Identify cost of an incident if the vulnerability were exploited by a threat actor.
- Identify cost of mitigating a vulnerability.
- Identify any compensatory controls that may enhance and augment controls.

The results obtained during continuous monitoring activities should be considered with respect to any necessary updates to the System Security Plan (SSP) and to the POAM, since the Authorizing Official, Information System Owner, and Security Control Assessor will be using these plans to guide future security assessment activities.

Continuous Monitoring

Continuous monitoring is not identical for all security controls, nor is it performed at the same time or with the same frequency for all controls. The various activities of the ongoing continuous monitoring process may be executed in the following timeframes:

(1) Near real-time, which uses automated mechanisms such as a security operations center or Security Event Information Manager (SIEM) to process output from security "watchdog" components (e.g., firewall, IDS/IPS, security event monitors/security information monitors) and from security-aware system components (that may produce security-relevant notifications, audit records, or SYSLOG records), and to process audit trail data from all sources. Results of this processing must be sent, at a minimum, to the designated point of contact (such as an operation center analyst) for further consideration.

(2) Periodic. This is the analysis of data collected at a predetermined frequency that is specified in the Continuous Monitoring Plan. (See CCM Plan at end of this template). Assessments of controls may require the collection and analysis of system operations data. The collection of data and analysis for periodic monitoring may be facilitated (i.e., scheduled and executed) by an automated tool(s).

(3) On-demand or ad hoc as needed. Controls to be monitored on an on-demand basis should be listed in the set of controls identified. The collection and analysis of data may be performed by any qualified individual or job role acceptable to the organization and system owner. The actual security control assessments should be performed by the Security Control Assessor, however. If the ISSO does not assist in data collection, analysis, or control assessments, the results should also be reviewed by the ISSO.

Common security controls, which are security controls not under direct control of the system owner, system managers, and administrators, must be monitored similarly to the controls of the information system. They are outside of the system's authorization boundary (e.g., external networks, facilities management offices, human resources offices, shared/external service providers). They may be under control of a different part of the same organization or may be controlled by an external organization. They may be provided by an organizational infrastructure supporting the system. Common security controls inherited from other systems or connected networks need to be monitored and the results of monitoring must be made available to the system owner. This monitoring is the responsibility of the common control provider and must be coordinated by the authorizing official and the organization's

SAISO [SENIOR CYBERSECURITY LEADER] or other senior official.

Assessment of Security Controls

The assessment of security controls is part of the ongoing continuous monitoring process.

Security controls may be assessed by manual techniques or automated or semi-automated mechanisms. Manual techniques consist of:

- Examination or inspection of system documentation, physical environment facilities, or system configuration data;
- Interviews with knowledgeable personnel; and
- Manual execution of system applications or software-implemented functions from a graphical user interface or from an operating system command line.

Some of the controls of the Technical and Operational classes may be capable of being assessed in part by automated or semi-automated mechanisms that cause the controls to be executed, which test the controls. For example, the execution of a software application or hardware appliance to analyze audit data tests the control to review and analyze audit data. Semi-automated mechanisms are typically manually invoked and execute a system function that implements a security control(s).

The system information collected during continuous monitoring, and the information collected by automated mechanisms, must be analyzed with respect to the specific NCF security controls being monitored. The information collected may not map cleanly to individual security controls and may need to be (1) analyzed, (2) decomposed into a finer granularity of data, and then (3) further analyzed with respect to the applicable controls. For instance, audit data that is collected may be used to assess several of the Audit (AU) family controls.

Summary

The Monitoring Security Controls step of the RMF consists of four focus areas: (i) configuration management and control; (ii) risk or impact analysis; (iii) ongoing security control monitoring; and (iv) status reporting and documentation. In summary, an effective continuous monitoring program includes:

- Configuration management and control processes for the information system, including documenting changes to the information system, network, environment, or operational procedures,
- Security impact analysis on actual or proposed changes to the information system and operational environments,
- Assessment of selected security controls in accordance with predetermined priorities and frequencies specified in the Continuous Monitoring Plan,
- Security status reporting to appropriate organizational individuals,
- Active involvement by authorizing officials in the ongoing management of information system-related security risks, and

- Active involvement of the system owner, information owner(s)/steward(s), and ISSO in the ongoing management and awareness of the security aspects of the information system and the information maintained on the system.

Security Controls Selection Process

The authorization process for an information system provides two important elements for the continuous monitoring activity: (a) a required set of security controls that must be maintained, and (b) a set of known weaknesses that must be corrected or monitored (and documented in the POAM), which determines the level of controls assessment needed to evaluate the system security posture. These three elements can serve as a starting point for the selection of security controls to be monitored.

The controls currently identified in the POAM may be selected for monitoring because they are:

- Partially implemented or incomplete.
- Missing or not implemented due to one of the following reasons:
    - Risk-based decision[1], which means that the Authorizing Official has accepted the risk of not implementing the security control.
    - New requirement for control because of (a) a risk assessment indicating new threat(s), system vulnerabilities, or organizational vulnerabilities or (b) newly discovered system vulnerabilities or deficiencies.
    - Compensated control, which mitigates a risk by other means. The compensating control must be tracked and assessed with respect to the control it replaces.
- Deferred due to resource unavailability or technology constraints.

In addition, controls that were identified in the POAM but resolved within the current year must be selected for monitoring.

Top priority for control monitoring should be directed at:

- The security controls that have the greatest potential for change after implementation (i.e., volatility) or
- The controls that have been implemented based on the organization's POAM for the information system, or
- Mitigating controls implemented due to a POAM item.

Some controls must be assessed more frequently because of frequent changes or for other reasons as described in this section. Security control volatility is a measure of how frequently a control is likely to change during the system lifecycle. Volatility may result from the need to apply software patches or to implement risk mitigations. Greater resources need to be

---

[1] In certain instances, the system may not have the technical capability to implement a security control or the system owner may make a risk-based decision not to implement a control based on the cost or feasibility of implementing the control relative to risk.

applied to security controls deemed to be of higher volatility, as there is a higher return on investment for assessing security controls of this type.

In addition to the security controls selected based on the criteria above, security controls may be selected for Continuous Monitoring based on:

- Controls that have changed but did not warrant a full system re-authorization, and
- Controls that were not tested for the previous one-year period of Continuous Monitoring activity.

With the concurrence of the Authorizing Official, the system owner and ISSO shall select and schedule continuous monitoring activities based on the factors presented above. The Authorizing Official and the SAISO or other senior official must approve the selection of these controls. The Security Control Assessor is responsible for evaluating the effectiveness of the controls.

In the selection process, the system owner and ISSO shall ensure that the assessment subset that has been selected includes controls that meet the following guidelines:

- Selected controls should represent the managerial class, operational class, and technical class of security controls;
- Selected controls should represent each of the NCF security control families; and
- An organization-specified minimum number of controls should be assessed each year, such as at least 33%. of the controls set for the information system.

Common security controls must also be continuously monitored as explained in Table 1 presents the format of selected controls for continuous monitoring as presented in ATTACHMENT A.

Table 1. Selected Controls for Continuous Monitoring

1	2	3	4	5	6	7	8	9
Selected Control	Reason for Selection	Type of Monitoring	Frequency of Monitoring	Type of Assessment	Frequency of Assessment	POC	Special Handling Required	Comments

Table 2.   Selected Controls for Continuous Monitoring Column Descriptions

Column	Heading	Contents—How to Complete
1	Selected Control	The applicable NCF security control identifier that is to be monitored.
2	Reason for Selection	Selection of a control does not necessarily mean that there is a potential issue with the control. The control may have been selected as one of the approximately 33% to be monitored in one year.
3	Type of Monitoring	If monitoring of a technical system function or capability (provided by software, hardware or firmware) is performed by automated means including by vulnerability and penetration test tools, the function may need to be mapped into one of the NCF security controls.
4	Frequency of Monitoring	Frequency may reflect automatic monitoring or scheduled manual monitoring. For automated monitoring, frequency of monitoring may be specified in terms of when the automated mechanism executes to determine security status or performance. Automated monitoring may include the sampling of system parameters relative to security.
5	Type of Assessment (Method)	If monitoring is by automated means, results may need to be mapped into the applicable security control for assessment and reporting.
6	Frequency of Assessment	Frequency should be stated for assessment against NCF, not by evaluations initiated by an automated tool or security operations center.
7	POC	Name of the individual, organization name, or title of the position within the Organization that is responsible for the operation of the specific control.
8	Special Handling Required	Any special handling required when certain conditions are detected or special processing of data to perform assessment.
9	Comments	The comments column is used for additional detail or clarifications and must be used if there is a delay. Common control provider should be supplied here (or an additional column added for common control information). The "Comments" column should identify any other, non-budgetary obstacles and challenges to monitoring. Comments field may contain indication of

Column	Heading	Contents—How to Complete
		any POAMs identified during system monitoring or assessment.

Security Controls Monitoring

Each selected control should have a monitoring method identified for it. The method for each control may be specified in ATTACHMENT A. The methods for monitoring security controls may encompass manual techniques, automated system monitoring computer platforms, such as system/network management centers or consoles, and manually invoked tools, such as test tools and configuration management tools. For most of the Management and Operational classes of security controls defined in the NCF, the methods for monitoring them will be the same as those methods used for assessment for the initial authorization to operate. These methods are, for the most part, manual and consist of:

- Examination of the information system, network, organization, and common control providers' documentation;
- Interviews with key personnel who are familiar with the operation of the security control being evaluated; and
- Manual invocation of some Operational class controls for testing purposes by operating certain system functions or executed from an operating system command line.

For the Technical class controls and for some of the Operational controls, it will be possible to use automated or semi-automated (manually invoked) mechanisms rather than manual methods to monitor their effectiveness. Several automated mechanisms are currently available and employed in information systems and networks that can provide the information needed to evaluate the effectiveness of many of the controls.

The outcome of continuous monitoring may be a need to remediate identified deficiencies or vulnerabilities in a security control. Remediation involves changes to the system software or hardware or to operational procedures. All changes require that an impact analysis be performed to determine any impact to the system or organization. Proposed changes to the system must be submitted to the configuration management process. After remediation, additional controls may need to be monitored as well as the remedied control.

Analysis of Results of Continuous Monitoring

The system information collected during continuous monitoring, and in particular the information collected by automated mechanisms, must be analyzed with respect to the NCF security controls selected for monitoring. The information collected may not map cleanly to individual security controls and may need to be analyzed, decomposed into a finer granularity of data, and then further analyzed with respect to the applicable controls. Information analysis is typically performed using the assessment methods that were used for the initial controls assessment for the approval to operate.

Assessment of security controls shall represent an independent, qualitative, and objective assessment of the stated controls within the defined operational and security environment of the system under review.

All security controls applicable to an information system and its environment must be assessed prior to the initial authorization, and subsets of controls must be re-assessed during each year of the authorization period. Security control assessment methods include:

(1) Examination of:
   a. Information system and organization documentation including security policy and procedures documents, system design and architecture documents and diagrams, system operations and administration manuals, and SSP;
   b. System components by observing hardware and cabling and through infrastructure and network-oriented diagrams;
   c. System settings by observing system configuration files and administration displays; and
   d. Physical environment,

(2) Interviews with key personnel to discuss concerns or questions developed during the document analysis, and to determine the extent of compliance with the security control(s) being assessed;

(3) Active security controls testing (e.g., functional testing and penetration testing) and observation of system operation and operational environment. When reporting the results of testing through vulnerability or penetration testing, the system functions tested and reported on must be mapped into the applicable security controls.

After the assessment, tentative changes to the system should be formulated and an Impact Analysis performed on them. If the tentative changes or other changes (e.g., compensating controls) are implemented, a Risk Assessment should be undertaken. Risk will be assessed for each issue identified from continuous monitoring. Each discovered deficiency or vulnerability will be tracked by an organization-defined procedure (e.g., by using a tool or approach that documents whether the item is open or closed, how it was resolved, when it was resolved, and whether it required a POAM entry). The ISSO and Authorizing Official (or Authorizing Official Designated Representative) will acknowledge a review and approval of the issues resolved and issues open and being tracked.

The [COMPANY/ORGANIZATION] will hold the final records for assessment of continuous monitoring activities based on the Continuous Monitoring strategy. Approval of the Continuous Monitoring Plan acknowledges agreement with selected security controls and results from continuous monitoring activities. As stated above, resolution of security control deficiencies identified will be approved via the organization's review and approval procedure. The System Assessment Report must also be updated, as described in the next section.

Reporting Results of Continuous Monitoring
[This section specifies where the results of Continuous Monitoring are documented and delivered.]

The results of continuous monitoring including security controls assessments, impact analyses, risk analyses, and recommendations are presented in the form of security status reports to the authorizing official and Agency senior managers by the system owner. Additionally, these reports may be sent to the ISSO, Information System Security Manager (ISSM), system administrator, system owner, organization/enterprise security officer or POC, organizational security function (e.g., help desk or incident response team), or repository of security issues. At a minimum, the security status report should summarize key changes to the SSP, SAR, and POAM.

The results of security control re-assessments should be documented in the SAR. The results of continuous monitoring of common controls must also be included (or referenced) in the updated SAR produced during the system continuous monitoring process. Common security controls implemented by the service provider (i.e., the owner of the system or network) that are not applicable to the system do not need to be monitored or documented for the system.

As the security authorization process becomes more dynamic in nature, relying to a greater degree on the continuous monitoring aspects of the process, the ability to update the SAR frequently based on the assessment results of security controls from the Technical and Operational classes becomes a critical aspect of an organization's information security program. The critical information contained in the accreditation package (i.e., the SSP, the SAR, and the POAM) should be updated on an ongoing basis providing the authorizing official and senior Agency officials with a status of the security state of the information system.

With the use of automated support tools and effective organization-wide security program management practices, authorizing officials should be able to access the most recent documentation in the authorization package at any time to determine the current security state of the information system, to help manage risk, and to provide essential information for reauthorization decisions.

Plan Approval
[This section provides the form for the signatures of approving authorities of this Continuous Monitoring Plan.]

Signatory Authority

This Continuous Monitoring Plan was prepared for the exclusive use and in support of [COMPANY/ORGANIZATION]. This plan has been reviewed and approved as indicated by the signatures below. Approval of this plan acknowledges agreement with selected security controls and results from any continuous monitoring activities captured within the [ORGANIZATION'S-IDENTIFIED TOOL OR REPOSITORY].

This document will be updated on an annual basis as part of continuous monitoring activities.

_____   _____

[NAME], Information System Security Officer   Date

_____   _____

[Name], Security Control Assessor   Date

_____   _____

[Name], Authorizing Official   Date
[Agency]

[A signature line may also be present for the Authorizing Official Designated Representative if applicable.]

EXAMPLE

Selected Controls for Cybersecurity-Continuous Monitoring

Selected Control	Reason for Selection	Type of Assessment	Frequency of Monitoring	Type of Monitoring	Frequency of Assessment	POC	Special Handling Required	Comment/Remarks
	FISMA	E	Annual	Manual	Annual		N/A	At Least Annually
	C	E, T	Annual	Manual	Annual		N/A	At Least Annually
	C	T	Year #1	Manual	Once every 3 years		N/A	
	S	T	Monthly	Manual	Annual		N/A	
	S	T	Quarterly	Manual	Annual		N/A	
	S	T	Year #1	Manual	Once every 3 years		N/A	
	S	T	Year #1	Manual	Once every 3 years		N/A	
	S	E	Year #1	Manual	Once every 3 years		N/A	
	S	T	Year #1	Manual	Once every 3 years		N/A	
	S	T	Year #1	Manual	Once every 3 years		N/A	
	C	T	Year #1	Manual	Once every 3 years		N/A	

About the Author

Mr. Russo is an internationally published author, and his work has been published in four foreign languages in addition to English. He is a former Senior Information Security Engineer within the Department of Defense's (DOD) F-35 Joint Strike Fighter program. He has an extensive background in cybersecurity and is an expert in the Risk Management Framework (RMF) and DOD Instruction 8510 which implements RMF throughout the DOD and the federal government. He holds both a Certified Information Systems Security Professional (CISSP) certification and a CISSP in information security architecture (ISSAP). He holds a 2017 certification as a Chief Information Security Officer (CISO) from the National Defense University, Washington, DC. He retired from the US Army Reserves in 2012 as the Senior Intelligence Officer.

Mr. Russo's credentials in cybersecurity...

He is the former CISO at the Department of Education wherein 2016 he led the effort to close over 95% of the outstanding US Congressional and Inspector General cybersecurity shortfall weaknesses spanning as far back as five years.

Mr. Russo is the former Senior Cybersecurity Engineer supporting the Joint Medical Logistics Development Functional Center of the Defense Health Agency (DHA) at Fort Detrick, MD. He led a team of engineering and cybersecurity professionals protecting five major Medical Logistics systems supporting over 200 DOD Medical Treatment Facilities around the globe.

In 2011, Mr. Russo is certified by the Office of Personnel Management as a graduate of the Senior Executive Service (SES) Candidate program.

From 2009 through 2011, Mr. Russo was the Chief Technology Officer at the Small Business Administration (SBA). He led a team of over 100 IT professionals in supporting an intercontinental Enterprise IT infrastructure and security operations spanning 12-time zones; he deployed cutting-edge technologies to enhance SBA's business and information sharing operations supporting the small business community.   Mr. Russo was the first-ever Program Executive Officer (PEO)/Senior Program Manager in the Office of Intelligence & Analysis at Headquarters, Department of Homeland Security (DHS), Washington, DC. He was responsible for the development and deployment of secure Information and Intelligence support systems for OI&A to include software applications and systems to enhance the DHS *mission. He was responsible for the program management development lifecycle during his tenure at DHS.*

He holds a Master of Science from the National Defense University in Government Information Leadership with a concentration in Cybersecurity and a Bachelor of Arts in Political Science with a minor in Russian Studies from Lehigh University. He holds Level III Defense Acquisition certification in Program Management, Information Technology, and Systems Engineering. He has been a member of the DOD Acquisition Corps since 2001.

NOTES: